Anonymous

Ladhope Leaves, a Spring Garland for 1887

Anonymous

Ladhope Leaves, a Spring Garland for 1887

ISBN/EAN: 9783337091262

Printed in Europe, USA, Canada, Australia, Japan

Cover: Foto ©ninafisch / pixelio.de

More available books at **www.hansebooks.com**

Printed by T. & A. CONSTABLE, *Printers to Her Majesty.*

CONTENTS

		PAGE
ALLEN, GRANT.		
Only an Infect,	. . . . .	46
ANDERSON, ALEXANDER.		
The Sorrow of the Sea,	. . . .	40
Saint Mary's Lake,	. . . . .	83
BARING-GOULD, Rev. S.		
Old England in the Sea,	. . . . .	8
BARRON, Rev. DOUGLAS G.		
Dunnottar,	. . . . .	35
BRYDEN, Rev. JAMES H.		
The Vifion of Truth,	. . . .	63
COCHRANE, ROBERT.		
A Valley of Peace, .	. .	33
'DICK.'		
Life's Enigma, . .	. .	70

Contents

	PAGE
'EFFIE.'	
Retrospect, ...	17
FURLEY, CATHERINE GRANT—	
Time's Magic, ...	28
A Weaver's Song, ...	73
'J. B. SELKIRK.'	
Death in Yarrow, ...	24
Love's Flame, ...	80
KENNEDY, THOMAS.	
In Caddonfoot Churchyard, . . .	11
The Children's Picnic, ...	59
LANG, ANDREW.	
The Last Cast, ...	20
Martial in Town, ...	38
'M. G.'	
Little Jock Elliot, ...	30
At Earlstoun, ...	42
MORTON, MRS.	
Ye're nearer God, my Bairnie, . .	74
RUSKIN, JOHN.	
Ashestiel, ...	1

Contents

	PAGE
RUSSELL, JOHN.	
Agnes Brown,	54
SAXBY, Mrs.	
Out in the Storm,	52
Leal Heart lo'es lang,	78
VEITCH, Professor.	
The Seven Spears of Wedderburn,	13
WEBSTER, HUGH A.	
Love,	77
L'Envoi,	88

'What fashion will you wear the garland of?'
>> *Much Ado about Nothing.*

'I would I had some flowers o' the spring that might
Become your time of day.
>> Daffodils,
That come before the swallow dares, and take
The winds of March with beauty; violets, dim,
But sweeter than the lids of Juno's eyes
Or Cytherea's breath; pale primroses,
That die unmarried, ere they can behold
Bright Phœbus in his strength.'
>> *The Winter's Tale.*

ASHESTIEL.

(From ' Fors Clavigera,' by permiſſion of the Author.)

Brantwood, October 10th, 1883.

I NOW take up my immediate ſubject of enquiry, the effect upon Scott's own mind of the natural ſcenery of the native land he loved ſo dearly. His life, let me firſt point out to you, was, in all the joyful ſtrength of it, ſpent in the valley of the Tweed. Edinburgh was his ſchool and his office; but his home was always by Tweedſide: and more perfectly ſo, becauſe in three ſeveral places during the three clauſes of life. You muſt remember alſo the cottage at Laſſwade for the firſt years of marriage, and Sandy Knowe for his childhood; but, allowing to Smailholm Tower and Roslin Glen whatever collateral influence they may rightly claim over the babe and the bridegroom, the constant influences of home remain divided strictly into the three æras at Rosebank, Ashestiel, and Abbotsford.

Rosebank, on the lower Tweed, gave him his close knowledge of the district of Flodden Field: and his store of foot-traveller's interest in every glen of Ettrick, Yarrow, and Liddel-water.

The vast tract of country to which these streams owe their power is composed of a finely-grained dark and hard sandstone, whose steep beds are uniformly and simultaneously raised into masses of upland, which nowhere present any rugged or broken masses of crag, like those of our Cumberland mountains, and are rarely steep enough anywhere to break the grass by weathering; a moderate shaly—or, rather, gritty—slope of two or three hundred feet opposite Ashestiel itself, being notice-

Asheſtiel

able enough, among the rounded monotony of general form, to receive the ſeparate name of 'the Slidders.' Towards the bottom of a dingle, here and there, a few feet of broken bank may ſhow what the hills conſiſt of; but the great waves of them riſe againſt the horizon without a ſingle peak, creſt, or cleft to diſtinguiſh one from another, though in their true ſcale of mountain ſtrength heaved into heights of 1500 or 2000 feet; and covering areas of three or four ſquare leagues for each of the ſurges. The dark rock weathers eaſily into ſurface ſoil, which forms for the greater part good paſture, with interſperſed patches of heath or peat, and Liddesdale-way, ruſhy and ſedgy moorland, good for little to man or beaſt.

•   •   •   •

As I drove from Abbotsford to Aſheſtiel, Tweed and Ettrick were both in flood; not dun nor wrathful, but in the clear fulneſs of their perfect ſtrength; and from the bridge of Ettrick I ſaw the two ſtreams join, and the Tweed for miles down the vale, and the Ettrick for miles up among his hills,—each of them, in the multitude of their windleſs waves, a march of infinite light, dazzling,—interminable,—intervaled indeed with eddies of ſhadow, but, for the moſt part, gliding paths of funſhine, far-ſwept beſide the green glow of their level inches, the bleſſing of them, and the guard: —the ſtately moving of the many waters, more peaceful than their calm, only mighty, their rippled ſpaces fixed like orient clouds, their pools of pauſing current binding the ſilver edges with a gloom of amber and gold; and all along their ſhore, beyond the ſward, and the murmurous ſhingle, proceſſions of dark foreſt, in ſtrange majeſty of ſweet order, and unwounded grace of glorious age.

The houſe of Aſheſtiel itſelf is only three or four miles above this junction of Tweed and Ettrick. It has been ſorrowfully changed ſince Sir Walter's death, but the essential make and set of the former building can still be traced. There is more excuse for Scott's flitting to Abbotsford than I had guessed, for *this* house stands, conscious of the river rather than commanding it, on a brow of meadowy bank, falling so steeply to the water that nothing can be seen of it from the windows. Beyond, the pasture-land rises steep three or four hundred feet against the northern sky, while behind the house, south and east, the moorlands lift themselves in gradual distance to still greater height, so that virtually neither sunrise nor sunset can be seen from the deep-nested dwelling. A tricklet of stream wavers to and fro down to it from the moor, through a grove of entirely natural wood, — oak, birch, and ash, fantastic and bewildering, but nowhere gloomy or decayed, and carpeted with anemone. Between this wild avenue and the house the old garden remains as it used to be, large, gracious, and tranquil; its high walls swept round it in a curving line like a war rampart, following the ground; the fruit-trees, trained a century since, now with grey trunks a foot wide, flattened to the wall like sheets of crag; the strong bars of their living trellis charged, when I saw them, with clusters of green-gage, soft bloomed into gold and blue, and of orange-pink magnum bonum, and crowds of ponderous pear, countless as leaves. Some open space of grass and path, now all redesigned for modern needs, must always have divided the garden from what was properly the front of the house, where the main entrance is now, between advanced wings, of which only the westward one is of Sir Walter's time: its ground-floor being the drawing-room, with his own bedroom of equal size above, cheerful and luminous both, enfilading the house front with their large side windows, which commanded the sweep of Tweed down the valley, and some high masses of Ettrick Forest beyond, this view being now moſtly ſhut off by the oppoſite wing, added for ſymmetry! But Sir Walter ſaw it fair through the morning clouds when he roſe, holding himſelf, nevertheleſs, altogether regardleſs of it, when once at work. At Aſheſtiel and Abbotsford alike, his work-room is ſtrictly a writing-office, what windows they have being deſigned to admit the needful light, with an extremely narrow viſta of the external world. Courtyard at Abbotsford, and bank of young wood beyond: nothing at Aſheſtiel but the green turf of the oppoſite fells with the ſun on it, if ſun there were, and ſilvery ſpecks of paſſing ſheep.

J. Ruskin

OLD ENGLAND IN THE SEA.

A JUBILEE HYMN.

ROUND the rocks and reefs of Britain
    Chafes and wreathes the reſtleſs tide;
    Verdure-clad and crowned with flowers,
  Decorated as a bride,
God-preſerved, on ſtrong foundations,
Nobleſt midſt a thouſand nations,
    Stands old England in the Sea.

What though ſnow-flakes fall about her,
  Ocean threat to break his chain,
Heavens darken, tempeſts gather,
  Undiſmayed ſhe will remain.

Old England in the Sea

Faction fleeteth as the shower,
Skies will brighten, cease to lower
      O'er old England in the Sea.

Far away in distant regions,
   Wheresoever breezes blow,
Where the tropic sun is blazing,
   Where unthawed lies arctic snow,
More dispersed than any other,
Children yet, who claim as mother
      Dear old England in the Sea.

Thousand-strong, though unseen fibres
   Interpenetrating run
Through that scattered race, compacting
   All inseparably in one;
One as notes in chorus swelling,
Everywhere the triumph telling
      Of old England in the Sea.

Lo! this year in loyal Britain
    Gains our Queen her jubilee:
God preserve her! all the people
    Sing with unanimity.
Tell abroad the stirring story,
Spread throughout the world the glory,
    Of old England in the Sea.

S. Baring-Gould.

IN CADDONFOOT CHURCHYARD.

A SONNET.

BEAUTIFUL spot! thrice hallowed are the dead
    That slumber here midst Nature's loveliness;
Summer hath so her sweet enchantments spread
  That Death seems holier in abodes like this.
Only the wild bird's note, the hymning river,
    Break the hushed calm where thy lone sleepers lie,
Whilst, grouped around, the solemn hills seem ever
  Gazing in supplication to the sky.

What is all learned philosophy or creed
    To the pure simple faith that here finds birth?
Here, where the soul, in its unvarnished need,
    Turns to that little church, and feels that earth,
Even in this beauty, doth but gild the way
To where its longings seek still brighter day?

Thomas Kennedy.

THE SEVEN SPEARS OF WEDDERBURN.

AN INCIDENT IN BORDER STORY.

THE Seven Spears of Wedderburn,
    High ſtalwart lads are they;
And in the ſun and 'neath the moon
    Ride foremoſt to the fray.

In many a Border foray,
    O'er many a heather hill,
The Spears have glanced, one after one,
    From Blackadder to Till.

And when the ſun was weſtering
    On Flodden's creſted height,
The Seven Spears of Wedderburn
    Gave firſt ſhock in the fight.

The minions now of Albany
    Are preying on the land;
The Laird of Home is done to death,
    And D'Arcy hath command

In all the Merfe and Lothians,
    Where only Home fhould reign:
That Frenchman on his fleeteft fteed
    Shall ne'er win back again.

So hot and faft gay D'Arcy rides;
    Behind him hot rides he,
The youngeft Spear of Wedderburn
    Fierce o'er the benty lea.

Now but one leap to clear the hag,
    And the foremoft horfe has won;
Or the gallant with the comely face
    Looks no more on the fun.

One fatal plunge, and D'Arcy
    Is helpleſs in the moſs:
Now ſtay thee, Jeſu Saviour!
    With the comfort of the Croſs!

For a ruthleſs hand is on thee,
    Like a tiger in its ire;
And vengeance in the Borderer
    Burns with a lurid fire.

And now he turns and homeward rides,
    But from his ſaddle-bow
There dangles by its yellow locks
    A knightly face and brow,—

So loved of dames and damoſels
    In the gay Court of France,
Now ſtrung in gleeful triumph
    'Neath the ſavage Border lance.

And many a mourning maiden
   Has shed the bitter tear
For D'Arcy's fate, the gallant knight,
   And Beauty's Chevalier.

What shall be said of thee, young Home,
   And of thy deadly turn?
What shall wipe out the bloody stain
   On the Spear of Wedderburn?

J. Veitch.

RETROSPECT.

LOWLY bends the breeze-kissed grass,
    Fair that still and sunlit wood,
Drowsy breezes as they pass
    Woo my heart to dreamy mood.

Through the mazes of my dream—
    Dream of days that used to be—
At my feet Tweed's silver stream
    Makes the sweetest melody.

Sweet as music heard of old,
    In the golden years long gone;
Fair as then the flowers unfold,
    With a beauty all their own.

Unchanged! as when of old we met,
    Together trod this flowery way—
The trysting-spot of lovers yet;
    My love, ah me! long miles away.

Yet not long miles of space between,
    Or swiftly rolling seas divide;
A nameless sense of change unseen,
    Our hearts united—severed wide.

Hand-clasped we stood together here,
    And love between us strove in vain
To bring our sundered spirits near;
    We sadly watched in mutual pain.

'Farewell,' he said, and turned away;
    'Farewell,' I whispered, yet my heart,
All weak and human, would delay
    To take the truer, better part.

Retrospect

Ah, well I knew 'twas better so;
    Our parting moments should be brief;
Yet, all regretful, bid him go—
    Our hearts beat one in mutual grief.

The olden paths I tread alone,
    With tender memories haunted yet;
He seeks in distant lands unknown
    To banish memory's fond regret.

Effie.

THE LAST CAST.

THE ANGLER'S APOLOGY.

JUST one cast more! how many a year,
    Beside how many a pool and stream,
Beneath the falling leaves and sere,
    I've sighed, reeled up, and dreamed my dream!

Dreamed of the sport since April first,
    Her hands fulfilled of flowers and snow,
Adown the pastoral valleys burst
    Where Ettrick and where Teviot flow.

Dreamed of the singing showers that break,
    And sting the lochs, or near or far,
And rouse the trout, and stir 'the take'
    From Urigil to Lochinvar.

Dreamed of the kind propitious sky
  O'er Ari Innes brooding grey;
The sea-trout, rushing at the fly,
  Breaks the black wave with sudden spray!

* * * * *

Brief are man's days at best; perchance
  I waste my own, who have not seen
The castled palaces of France
  Shine on the Loire in summer green.

And clear and fleet Eurotas still,
  You tell me, laves his reedy shore,
And flows beneath his fabled hill
  Where Dian drave the chase of yore.

And 'like a horse unbroken' yet
  The yellow stream with rush and foam,
'Neath tower, and bridge, and parapet,
  Girdles his ancient mistress, Rome!

I may not see them, but I doubt,
    If seen, I'd find them half so fair
As ripples of the rising trout
    That feed beneath the elms of Yair.

Nay, Spring I'd meet by Tweed or Ail,
    And Summer by Loch Assynt's deep,
And Autumn in that lonely vale
    Where wedded Avons westward sweep,

Or where, amid the empty fields,
    Among the bracken of the glen,
Her yellow wreath October yields
    To crown the crystal brows of Ken.

Unseen, Eurotas, southward steal,
    Unknown, Alpheus, westward glide,
You never heard the ringing reel,
    The music of the water-side!

The Laſt Caſt

Though gods have walked your woods among,
    Though nymphs have fled your banks along ;
You ſpeak not that familiar tongue
    Tweed murmurs like my cradle ſong.

My cradle ſong,—nor other hymn
    I'd chooſe, nor gentler requiem dear
Than Tweed's, that through death's twilight dim
    Mourned in the lateſt Minſtrel's ear !

Andrew Lang.

DEATH IN YARROW.

IT 'S no the fax month gane
　　Sin' a' our cares began,
　Sin' fhe left us here alane,
　　Her callant and gudeman.
It was in the Spring fhe dee'd,
　　And now we're in the fa';
And fair we 've ftruggled wi't,
　　Sin' his mother gaed awa'.

An awfu' blow was that—
　　The deed that nane can dree;
And lang and fair we grat
　　For her we couldna fee.
I 've aye been ftrong and fell,
　　And can ftand a gey bit thraw;

Death in Yarrow.

But the laddie's no his fel'
   Sin' his mother gaed awa'.

In a' the water-gate
   Ye couldna find his marrow;
There wasna' ane his mate
   In Ettrick Shaws or Yarrow.
But he hasna' now the look
   He used to hae ava;
He's grown sae little buik
   Sin' his mother gaed awa'.

I tak' him on my back
   In ilka blink o' sun,
Rin roun' about the stack,
   And mak' believe it's fun.
But weel he kens, I warrant,
   There's something wrang for a',
He's turned sae auld-farrant
   Sin' his mother gaed awa'.

For when he's played his fill,
    I canna help but fee
How he draws the creepie-ftool
    Aye the clofer to my knee ;
And he turns his muckle een
    To the pictur' on the wa',
Wi' a face grown thin and keen
    Sin' his mother gaed awa'.

I mak' his pickle meat—
    And I think I mak' it weel ;
And I warm his little feet
    When I hap him i' the creel ;
And he kiffes me fu' couthie,
    For he downa' fleep at a'
Till he hauds up his bit mouthie,
    Sin' his mother gaed awa'.

And then I dander oot
    When I can do nae mair,

And walk the hills aboot,
    I dinna aye ken where;
For my hairt's wi' ane abune,
    And the ane is growin' twa,
He's dwined sae fair, sae sune,
    Sin' his mother gaed awa'.

And now the lang day's dune,
    And the nicht's begun to fa',
And a bonnie harvest mune
    Rises up on Bowerhope Law.
It's a bonnie warlt this,
    But it's no for me at a',
For a'thing's gane amiss
    Sin' his mother gaed awa'.

J. B. Selkirk.

TIME'S MAGIC.

SORROW'S difcords I have known
    Rhythmic grow at touch of time;
What was once a piteous groan
    Help to make a dainty rhyme.

Rocks that one time barred my way,
    Thorns that tore me as I paffed,
Seen by light of dying day
    Make a picture at the laft.

Say not, in this life of mine,
    This was grievous, that was wrong;
Sorrow by a law divine
    Is the chofen feed of fong.

Time's Magic

True it is the griefs were great,
    True it is the songs are small;
Yet the verses compensate
    For the troubles after all.

Tones that seem too harsh to-day
    Make life's harmony complete;
Yet I do not dare to say
    Whether life is sad or sweet.

Catherine Grant Furley.

LITTLE JOCK ELLIOT.

MY caſtle is aye my ain,
  An' herried it never ſall be;
For I maun fa' ere it's taen,
  An' wha daur meddle wi' me?
Wi' my kute i' the rib o' my naig,
  My ſwurd hingin' doun by my knee,
For man I am never afraid—
  For wha daur meddle wi' me?

  Wha daur meddle wi' me?
  Wha daur meddle wi' me?
  Oh, my name it is Little Jock Elliot,
    An' wha daur meddle wi' me?

Little Jock Elliot

Fierce Bothwell I vanquiſhed clean,
    Gar'd troopers an' fitmen flee;
By my faith, I dumfoondert the Queen;
    But wha daur meddle wi' me?
Alang by the Dead-Water Stank,
    Jock Fenwick I met on the lea,
But his ſaddle was toom in a clank;
    An' wha daur meddle wi' me?

Where Keeldar meets wi' the Tyne,
    Myſel' an' my kinſmen three,
We tackled the Percys nine—
    They'll never mair meddle wi' me.
Sir Harry, wi' nimble brand,
    He pricket my cap ajee,
But I cloured his head on the ſtrand—
    An' wha daur meddle wi' me?

The Cumberland rievers ken
    The ſtraike my arm can gie,

An' warily pafs the glen—
　　For wha daur meddle wi' me?
I've chafed the loons doun to Carlifle,
　　Jooket the raip on the Hairibee,
Where my naig nickert an' cocket his tail—
　　But wha daur meddle wi' me?

My kinfmen are true, an' brawlie,
　　At glint o' an enemie,
Round Parke's auld turrets they rally,
　　An' wha daur meddle wi' me?
Then heigh for the tug an' the tuffle,
　　Though the coft be Jethart tree;
Let the Queen an' her troopers gae whuffle!
　　Oh, wha daur meddle wi' me?
　　　　Wha daur meddle wi' me?
　　　　Wha daur meddle wi' me?
　　　　Oh, my name it is Little Jock Elliot,
　　　　　An' wha daur meddle wi' me?

　　　　　　　　　　　　M. G.

A VALLEY OF PEACE.

WE sat at Heaven's Gate one Sabbath-day,
    Glory from out the inner splendour flowed,
  Which lit the mountains, and the valleys glowed
A golden channel for the river's way.

Sunlight above, and the green vale below,
    Our hearts were quiet, smitten through and
        through
  By gentle peace, which, falling as the dew,
Was soft as a sweet sunset's afterglow.

We crept to church across a wild-wood hill,
    And down the valley to the meeting-place,
  Where footsteps echoed, ere the preacher's face
Bade all be silent 'neath a Higher will.

The meſsage came, a holy, happy word;
    And ſo, refreſhed, home through the ſultry noon,
    Which now for us with many joys was ſtrewn,
Like opening ſpring with carol of the bird.

Noon fell to evening, evening ſoft and calm
    Fell round the day in glory of weſtern fire;
    When folded in, each hope and each defire
Sank quiet as the woods then breathing balm.

So would we ever ſit at Heaven's Gate,
    That, when the voices from the world grow loud,
    Our ſpirits, bathed in ſilence, may be bowed,
In lowly patience on God's will to wait.

Robert Cochrane.

DUNNOTTAR.

[In Dunnottar Churchyard are the graves of the Covenanters who perished in Dunnottar Castle in 1685.]

ON the dim churchyard, cold and grey,
    Where nobler feet than mine have trod,
I mused alone at fall of day,
    And wondered at the ways of God—
The shift and stir of things most still,
    The changes that are sure to come:
Be moved, thou everlasting hill!
    Thou clarion voice of Truth, be dumb!
      The voice is hushed, and silently
      The mountain falls into the sea.

And here in common slumbers bound,
    They sleep, the pride of bygone days,

Nameless beneath their burial mound,
  Or marked by word of wonted praise.
How close they gather to their rest:
  Grim earls who fought for king and crown,
And knaves who deemed confusion best,
  And traders tired of shop and town,
    And fisher-folks, whose dream must be
    Of brown sails bending o'er the sea.

And last, but surely first in love,
  We place the names of those who fell
Their faith in direst strait to prove:
  God gave them peace who fought so well;
The hallowed peace they pray'd to win,
  And welcomed with their parting breath;
The peace that purged a nation's sin,
  And brought to each a martyr's death:
    Their blood a witness sure should be,
    And lasting as the eternal sea.

Dunnottar

Ah, well, 'tis much that they have been,
  Though we are milder, wifer grown,
And fkill'd, perchance, to read between
  The broken lines on yonder ftone.
We judge by what we are and feel,
  Who move beyond the ftrain and ftir
That roufed of old the fiery zeal
  Of Prelate and of Prefbyter.
    Now here, from unbleft hatreds free,
    They fleep together by the fea.

But when the fands of time are run,
  And all our little changes fped,
And ftanding 'neath the broad white fun
  Chrift bids the grave give up its dead;
Though kings may rife and pafs unknown,
  Too mean to walk at God's right hand,
Methinks befide the Father's Throne
  Himfelf will place that faithful band,
    And fay, Behold, they died for Me
    In yon old dungeon by the fea.

Douglas G. Barron.

MARTIAL IN TOWN.

LAST night, within the ſtifling train,
    Lit by the foggy lamp o'erhead,
    Sick of the ſad Laſt News, I read
Verſe of that joyous child of Spain,

Who dwelt when Rome was waxing cold,
    Within the Roman din and ſmoke,
    And like my heart to me they ſpoke,
Theſe accents of his heart of old:—

  Brother, had we but time to live,
    And fleet the careleſs hours together,
  With all that leiſure has to give
    Of perfect life and peaceful weather,

Martial in Town

The Rich Man's halls, the anxious faces,
The weary Forum, courts, and cafes
   Should know us not; but quiet nooks,
But summer shade by field and well,
   But country rides, and talk of books,
At home, with these, we fain would dwell!

Now neither lives, but day by day
   Sees the suns wasting in the west,
And feels their flight, and doth delay
   To lead the life he loveth best.

So from thy city prison broke,
   Martial, thy wail for life misspent,
And so, through London's noise and smoke
   My heart replies to the lament.

For dear as Tagus with his gold,
   And swifter Salo, were to thee,
So dear to me the woods that fold
   The streams that circle Fernielea!

                            Andrew Lang.

THE SORROW OF THE SEA.

 DAY of fading light upon the sea,
    Of sea-birds winging to their rocky caves;
And ever with its monotone to me,
    The sorrow of the waves.

They leap and lash among the rocks and sands,
    White-lipped, as with a guilty secret tossed,
For ever feeling with their foamy hands
    For something they have lost.

Far out, and swaying in a sweet unrest,
    A boat or two against the light is seen,
Dipping their sides within the liquid breast
    Of waters dark and green.

The Sorrow of the Sea

And farther still, where sea and sky have kissed,
   There falls, as if from heaven's own threshold, light
Upon faint hills that, half-enswathed in mist,
   Wait for the coming night.

But still, though all this life and motion meet,
   My thoughts are wingless and lie dead in me,
Or dimly stir to answer at my feet
   The sorrow of the sea.

Alexander Anderson.

AT EARLSTOUN.

A LOVELY moon through clouds of snow
  Her tender light is streaming
On wood and hill and plain below,
  And brook like silver gleaming;
And many a scene around me lies
  On which I love to ponder,
When Night, loved Night, with pearly eyes,
  Invites me forth to wander.

The owl from Rhymer's mouldering tower
  A dreary cry is pealing,
While neighbouring cliff and glen and bower
  Their echoes are revealing;

At Earlstoun

And distant murmurings come and go—
    The soft winds sadly sighing
O'er Cowdenknowes, where, drooping low,
    The bonnie broom is dying.

Round yonder hill, in softest light,
    Fair Melrose now reposes,
Where Tweed unto the queen of night
    His glittering wealth discloses;
And silent as a waveless sea,
    A silent vigil keeping,
Stands Dryburgh's hallowed pile, where he,
    The mighty Bard, is sleeping.

The moonlit hills in slumber lie,
    And dreamlike fill the distance,
And mingle with the clouds till sky
    And earth have one existence;

And mingle with the clouds as though
    With heaven they held communion,
While peace from hill to vale below
    Holds undisturbed dominion.

And with the tender light, so fair,
    On cloud and landscape breaking,
A mystic influence fills the air,
    The heart and soul awaking;
Till, glimmering like the stars of night,
    Strange memories rise before me,
And thoughts that only come when bright
    The still moon floateth o'er me:

Bright thoughts, the spirit-land their goal,
    That come and go unspoken,
And memories that perplex the soul,
    So interlinked and broken.

At Earlstoun

And though the Night's impressive power
    May touch a spring of sadness,
Its mild accordance with the hour
    Falls on the heart like gladness.

So with the hours that speed the night
    I trace the hill, the meadow,
And linger 'mid the chequered light,
    The dreamy light and shadow;
Reluctant from a scene to part
    I so devoutly cherish,
Though in the chambers of my heart
    Its image ne'er can perish.

M. G.

ONLY AN INSECT.

I.

ON the crimſon cloth
    Of my ſtudy deſk,
A luſtrous moth
    Poiſed ſtatueſque.
Of a waxen mould
    Were its light limbs ſhaped,
And in ſcales of gold
    Its body was draped:
While its luminous wings
    Were netted and veined
With ſilvery ſtrings,
    Or golden-grained,

Only an Insect

Through whose filmy maze
   In tremulous flight
Danced glittering rays
   Of the gladsome light.

II.

On the desk hard by
   A taper burned,
Towards which the eye
   Of the insect turned.
In its vague little mind
   A faint desire
Rose, undefined,
   For the beautiful fire.
Lightly it spread
   Each silken van;
Then away it sped
   For a moment's span.
And a strange delight
   Lured on its course

With refiftlefs might
　　Toward the central fource:
And it followed the fpell
　　Through an eddying maze,
Till it fluttered and fell
　　In the deadly blaze.

III.

Dazzled and ftunned
　　By the fcalding pain,
One moment it fwooned,
　　Then rofe again;
And again the fire
　　Drew it on with its charms
To a living pyre
　　In its awful arms;
And now it lies
　　On the table here
Before my eyes,
　　Shrivelled and fere.

Only an Insect

IV.

As I sit and muse
   On its fiery fate,
What themes abstruse
   Might I meditate!
For the pangs that thrilled
   Through its delicate frame
As its senses were filled
   With the scorching flame,
A riddle enclose
   That, living or dead,
In rhyme or in prose,
   No seer has read.
'But a moth,' you cry,
   'Is a thing so small!'
Ah, yes; but why
   Should it suffer at all?
Why should a sob
   For the vaguest smart

One moment throb
   Through the tinieſt heart?
Why, in the whole
   Wide univerſe,
Should a ſingle ſoul
   Feel that primal curſe?
Not all the throes
   Of mightieſt mind,
Nor the heavieſt woes
   Of humankind,
Are of deeper weight
   In the riddle of things
Than that inſect's fate
   With the mangled wings.

v.

But if only I
   In my ſimple ſong
Could tell you the Why
   Of that one little wrong,

Only an Insect

I could tell you more
    Than the deepest page
Of saintliest lore
    Or of wisest sage.
For never as yet
    In its wordy strife
Could Philosophy get
    At the import of life:
And Theology's saws
    Have still to explain
The inscrutable cause
    For the being of pain.
So I somehow fear
    That in spite of both,
We are baffled here
    By this one singed moth.

Grant Allen.

OUT IN THE STORM.

WHEN the winds and the waves have wakened
   To echo each other's moan,
When the ships are speeding to harbour,
   She stands on the shore alone;
Around her the storm-clouds gather,
   And the white squall spreads its wings,
And the clamour of warring forces.
   From the soul of the tempest springs.

Oh, wild and wide are the surges,
   And strong are the powers of the air;
And God—He knows, and none other,
   What the human heart can bear.

Out in the Storm

The fear, and the hope, and the longing
    Stir in her a vague unrest;
For the boy who was rocked on her bosom
    Is borne on the ocean's breast.

But far as the waves can wander,
    As fast as the winds can fly,
From the deepest depths of the ocean
    To the highest heights of the sky,
Through the tears of a lonely vigil,
    Through the gloom of a dumb despair,
To the ear of a pitying Father
    Is wafted a mother's prayer.

Jessie M. E. Saxby.

AGNES BROWN.

[Died 14th January 1820, aged eighty-eight; buried in Bolton Churchyard, near Haddington.]

THE spring birds sing, nor care if no one listen,
    The spring flowers open if the sun but shine,
The spring winds wander where the green buds glisten,
    Through all the vale of Tyne.

And while, to music of the spring's returning,
    Thy fair stream, Gifford, in the sunlight flows,
I, nursing tender thoughts, this sweet March morning,
    Stand where the dead repose.

The snowdrop on the grass-green turf is blowing,
  Its pure white chalice to the cold earth hung;
The crocus with its heart of fire is glowing
  As when old Homer sung.

And round me are the quaint-hewn gravestones, giving,
  With emblem rude, by generations read,
Their simple words of warning for the living,
  Of promise for the dead.

But not that mausoleum, huge and hoary,
  With elegiac marble, telling how
Its long-forgotten great ones died in glory,
  Has drawn me hither now.

Ah, no!—With reverence meet from these I turn:
  They had what wealth could bring or love supply,
Like thousands such, who, born as they were born,
  Live, have their day, and die.

Let peace be theirs! It is a fairer meed,
    A more enduring halo of renown,
That glorifies this grave, o'er which I read
    The name of AGNES BROWN.

A peasant name, befitting peasant tongue:
    How lives it longer than an autumn moon?
'Twas hers, the mother of the Bard who sung
    The banks and braes of Doon.

Here in this alien ground her ashes lie,
    Far from her native haunts on Carrick shore,
Far from where first she felt a mother's joy
    O'er the brave child she bore.

Ah, who can tell the thoughts that on her prest,
    As o'er his cradle-bed she bent in bliss,
Or gave from the sweet fountains of her breast
    The life that nourished his?

Agnes Brown

Perhaps in prescient vision came to her
    Some shadowings of the glory yet afar—
Of that fierce storm, whence rose, serene and clear,
    His never-setting star.

But dreamt she ever, as she sang to still
    His infant heart in slumber sweet and long,
That he who silent lay the while, should fill
    Half the round world with song?

Yet so he filled it; and she lived to see
    The Singer, chapleted with laurel, stand,
Upon his lips that wondrous melody
    Which thrilled his native land.

She saw, too, when had passed the Singer's breath,
    A nation's proud heart throbbing at his name,
Forgetting, in the pitying light of death,
    Whatever was of blame.

Ladhope Leaves

Oh, may we hope she heard not, even afar,
    The screamings of that vulture-brood who tear
The heart from out the dead, and meanly mar
    The fame they may not share!

Who would not wish that her long day's decline
    Had peacefullest setting, unsuffused with tears,
Who bore to Scotland him, our Bard divine,
    Immortal as the years?

He sleeps among the eternal; nothing mars
    His rest, nor ever pang to him returns:
Write, too, her epitaph among the stars,
    MOTHER OF ROBERT BURNS!

John Russell.

THE CHILDREN'S PICNIC.

THEY are romping about, the darlings,
    Through the tufted grafs and the flowers;
God blefs them, the innocent darlings,
    In the glee of their joyous hours!
There is funfhine without, they have funfhine within,
And their glad hearts pour mufic in laughter and din;
Let them feaft of life's joys ere its battles begin,
    Or the cloud of its troubling lowers.

The foft fummer winds are playing
    With the links of their waving hair,

And on each flushed cheek are laying
   The tints of the roses fair;
And innocence, jubilant, looks from their eyes,
Whose brightness makes brighter the cheek's ruddy
   dyes:
Alas! that ripe years should bring sadness and sighs,
   And wither the blossoming there.

Oh, my spirit leaps light with you, darlings,
   And fain would I join in your glee,
But that one who was once like you, darlings,
   With pale face forbids it to be!
Far down in my heart's holiest memories, two eyes,
Whose light is the light of no earthly skies,
Through the glistening tear that there death-frozen
   lies,
   Imploringly looketh to me.

And I turn me away from you, darlings,
   For a sickness is filling my breast,

And my griefs that have flumbered long, darlings,
   Are breaking again from their reft.
I turn to the folitudes, there to conceal
The emotions too tender and pure to reveal,
Where, with Nature alone, my bruifed fpirit may kneel,
   And its troubles and woes be confeft.

Yet rejoice in your merriment, darlings,
   Think not of this grieving of mine;
This world ftill is beautiful, darlings,
   So let its pure pleafures be thine.
God's love's in the funfhine that gladdens the hills,
In the fongs of the birds, in the flowers and the rills,
Then fhout in your joy, for their influence that fills
   Your young hearts with delight is divine.

Thomas Kennedy.

THE VISION OF TRUTH.

 SAT beside a rippling stream,
    The air was bright and pure and warm,
Without a jarring sound to harm
The pensive stillness of my dream.

I thought myself again a youth,
    I thought of days, now long gone by,
    When, filled with aspirations high,
I wandered forth in quest of Truth.

I sought her in what sages said;
    And in the books they left behind—
    Rich products of the human mind—
I held communion with the dead.

The Vision of Truth

I sought her where, ere half his age,
    Old Scotia's poet breathed his last;
    And where, with his conceptions vast,
There lived and wrote the 'Chelsea sage.'

I sought her 'mid the sacred shrines
    Where Stratford's marvellous poet lies;
    I sought her where, with sightless eyes,
The British Homer penned his lines.

And, weary of my native shore,
    Where wealth appeared the leading aim,
    Or eager thirst for transient fame,
Which, never sated, cries for more,

I sought her where the dew distils
    On Luther's grave, on Goethe's home;
    I sought her where eternal Rome
Stands proudly on her seven hills.

I fought her in that city's halls
    Where Socrates and Plato stood
    Together in their search for good,
And taught the youth within its walls.

I sought her in that sacred land,
    Most blest, I thought, on earth below,
    Where, all who read the Scriptures know,
The Master trained His little band.

I sought to know the Brahmin's creed,
    What Buddha taught in ancient times,
    And what men thought in sunny climes
Where Zoroaster taught the Mede.

I sought her in that country, full
    Of people wondrous from of old,
    And where, even yet, 'tis proudly told,
Confucius taught the 'golden rule.'

The Vision of Truth

I found her not.   At least I thought
   I should the light more clearly see;
   I longed to leave the earth, and flee
To find out that fair form I sought.

Again I homeward bent my way,
   Again I oped the well-known door,
   And to the murmuring sea once more
I listened as in youth's bright day.

And sitting in my father's chair,
   I mused upon my little life;
   What meaneth all the mortal strife,
The gnawing pain, the secret care?

I asked myself, in growing fear,
   What fate can be in store for those
   Whose lives begin, continue, close,
Without a thought of God to cheer?

I lost myself in mazy trance,
    The vastness overwhelmed my soul,
    As, thinking of the worlds that roll,
I felt my insignificance.

I sank as in a billowy sea,
    With dread annihilation nigh,
    And from my soul arose the cry,
'Let there be light, if light there be.'

And, lo, like vision of the night,
    As if in answer to my prayer,
    Appeared a Being wondrous fair,
And clothed with more than earthly light.

'My son,' she said, with gentle voice,
    'You sought me far, you sought me wide,
    And now you see me by your side,
Rise up then, Doubter, and rejoice.

The Vision of Truth

' You sought me well; you have done right
 To search for me; where'er they go,
 The highest quest that men can know
Is Truth, in all her beauty bright.

' The meaning full you do not know
 Of that one struggling, painful life,
 Of that one death 'mid fiendish strife,
Which Love Divine endured below.

' Shut in by Nature's boundary line,
 You cannot, with your feeble sense,
 Pretend to know Omniscience,
Or measure out the mind Divine.

' But when you see the perfect whole,
 Of all its present mystery bared,
 You then will wonder that you dared
To doubt the great, unerring Soul,

' That watches o'er the sparrow's fall,
    That guides the insect, tends the flower,
    Whose justice, goodness, love, and power
Are everywhere, are all in all.

' Think truly ; there the secret lies
    Of noble deeds, of purpose sure,
    Of lives exalted, noble, pure,
The strength of all the great and wise.

' Know well thyself : the man who strives
    The hearts and souls of men to reach,
    Must from his own experience teach
The secret of all noble lives.

' Strive ever to attain the true,
    As onward in your life you move,
    Till in complete and perfect love
You live with me, and I with you.

The Vision of Truth

'My name is Truth, and Truth is Love,
   And Love is God, and God is all;
   Believe in this, you will not fall;
And trust me where you cannot prove.'

The vision fled; her words remained;
   I rose a new, an altered man;
   I saw a glimpse of one great plan,
And faith, and hope, and peace regained.

And so my dark forebodings fell;
   And in the evening of my life
   I look beyond the sin and strife,
And rest in this, that 'all is well.'

James H. Bryden.

LIFE'S ENIGMA.

ONLY a long deep silence,
    And a mist that's over the heart;
And the world is full of the shadows
    That out of my dreamland start.

Away are the keen heart-longings,
    And away on an unseen track;
For I listen the live-long morrow,
    And they bring me no answer back.

And the mist winds round me closer,
    And the silence is ill to bear,

Life's Enigma

And the soul looks out on the twilight,
    Weary and wan with its care.

For it hears the wind-voice sighing
    Where the long pine-branches wave,
And it ever speaks to the spirit
    Of the past that's laid in the grave.

And the sad strains waken yearning,
    A yearning that will not be;
And the sense that I cannot fathom
    Comes out of my Life to me.

And I stand in the great Creation,
    Like a child by the altar-stair,
While the grand eternal anthem
    Dies into the plaintive prayer.

For I cannot grasp life's meaning,
    Or tell of the smallest thing;
And the higher I climb, the deeper
    The mysteries round me cling.

And I stand in the great Creation
    Like a child by the mighty sea;
And what of the depths when the shallows
    Are more than enough for me?

And ever it comes; and ever,
    The more that I see, seems the less
The knowledge of Life and of Being,
    Of earth and its earnestness.

Dick.

A WEAVER'S SONG.

To and fro, to and fro,
    With its swift rebound doth the shuttle go;
The warp-threads rise, the warp-threads fall,
Till a quaint fair pattern binds them all.
Early and late, early and late,
Slender warp-thread and woof-thread mate.

To and fro, to and fro,
The shuttle of Chance through our life doth go;
Our passions are threads that rise and fall,
Till a strange sad pattern binds them all.
Early and late, early and late,
The shuttle of Chance weaves the web of Fate.

Catherine Grant Furley.

YE'RE NEARER GOD, MY BAIRNIE.

YE 'RE nearer God, my bairnie,
    Than when ye were wi' me;
An' though we noo hae pairtit,
    It's only for a wee.

An' ilka nicht that I lie doon,
    Before I steek my e'e,
My heart gies thanks that I hae come
    A day's march nearer thee.

Ower guid wert thou, my bairnie!
    Ower guid to bide wi' me;
I only got ye, bairnie,
    To *haud* ye for a wee.

An' while I held ye to my heart,
    Sae dear wert thou to me,
I thocht if ye were afkit back—
    My bairnie!—I wad dee.

I wearied for the funny days,
    I wearied for them fair;
I watch'd the dreary winter-clouds
    Wi' filent dread an' care.

Dark fears cam' creepin' ower me,
    Whan cam' the froft an' fnaw;
But bitter, bitter woe was mine
    Before they gaed awa.

'Twas awfu' fair, my bairnie,
    'Twas awfu' fair to pairt;
An' oh! it 's awfu' fair to live,
    An' hae a broken heart!

But safe are ye, my bairnie!
    The gentle heart o' thine
Will never, never ken the woe
    That wrings this heart o' mine.

The warld 's noo dark, my bairnie,
    It 's dark an' drear to me,
For gane is a' the happiness
    That I hae haen wi' thee.

Although I ken ye 're faulded safe,
    An' Wisdom says to me,
That I 'sud gladly thole what 's gien
    Sic happiness to thee,'

It 's ill to see through blindin' tears
    A truth sae fair to learn;
Fain, fain wad I hae keepit thee,
    My bonnie, bonnie bairn!

Jessie D. M. Morton.

LOVE.

A SONNET.

As one who, scanning close the midnight sky,
　Where holds each orb its own appointed place,
　Should haply chance, by fortune's special grace,
When least he hoped such wonder, to descry
Some star unseen before by mortal eye,
　And, having seen it for a little space,
　Should straightway lose thereof all sight and trace;
But soul-enamour'd of its matchless dye,
　Should heed no more at all the meaner crew

Of nightly stars that hold their steadfast state,
>   But gaze and gaze unwearied all night through
At one small patch of darkness, hoping fate
>   Would bring once more that one sole star to view:—
Even so I saw thy love, and so I wait.

Hugh A. Webster.

LEAL HEART LO'ES LANG.

OH, the soft wind sighed o'er the graffy knowe,
    Where the wee birds warbled fweet,
And the rofes bloomed upon ilka bough,
    And the days were fair as fleet;
And the laddie lilted a dream-taught fang:
    'Leal heart lo'es lang.'

Under the roots o' the wild-rofe tree
    They laid the puir lad to reft,
And the low winds moaned frae the fcented lea,
    And the birdies built a neft;
And the birds, and the breeze, and the bloffoms fang,
    'Leal heart lo'es lang.'

Nae dreams had he there; but when years were
    gane,
  She came by that quiet place;
Her steps they were slow, and she gaed her lane,
  And pale was her faded face:
And the tear-drops fell as she sadly sang,
  'Leal heart lo'es lang.'

Jessie M. E. Saxby.

LOVE'S FLAME.

COME, Shepherd, now my lute's in tune,
    What would you I ſhould ſing or play?
Some meaſure laden ſweet as June
    With languorous odours? Tell me, pray.
Some air to trickle through your ſoul,
Like dewdrops in the roſe's bowl?
    No! ſay'ſt thou ſo?
Ah then, love's tender flame,
Thou haſt not known, perhaps, except in name!

At gloaming by that pleaſant rill
    Which murmurs to the murmuring ſhore,
Haſt never waited on the hill
    Beneath the ſpreading ſycamore,

And, liſtening for her coming feet,
Heard through thy lips thine own heart beat?
    No! ſay'ſt thou ſo?
Ah then, love's quivering flame,
Thou haſt not known it, Shepherd, but in name!

Haſt never met by ford or field
    That maiden, freſh and free from blame,
Beneath whoſe gaze thy pulſes reeled
    With ſenſe of unaccuſtomed ſhame?
And when to ſpeak you would have come,
Found ſuddenly that you were dumb!
    No! ſay'ſt thou ſo?
Ah then, love's conquering flame
Thou haſt not known as yet, except in name!

Say, haſt thou never heard a voice
    That ſeemed to you ſo ſtrange and new,
It made all other ſounds but noiſe
    Compared to that you liſtened to?

Love's Flame.

As if it held in every breath
The iſſues of your life or death?
    No! ſay'ſt thou ſo?
Ah then, love's piercing flame,
Thou never canſt have known it but in name!

Shepherd, adieu! my ſong is done!
    Go to thy bacon and thy beans;
Why ſhould I ſing or play to one
    Who does not know what Muſic means?
'Tis love's own language, and as yet
You do not know your alphabet;
    No! Shepherd, no!
To you, love's tender flame
Has never been revealed, except in name!

J. B. Selkirk.

SAINT MARY'S LAKE.

AWAY from all the reſtleſs ſtreet,
    The whirlpool of the toiling race,
Where Traffic, in the duſty heat,
    Toils with the ſweat upon his face.

Away from this, and far away,
    We fight the ſtrong wind on the hill,
Or reſt upon the bracken'd brae,
    And ſhape our dreamland as we will.

What boon to lie, as now I lie,
    And ſee in ſilver at my feet
Saint Mary's Lake, as if the ſky
    Had fallen between thoſe hills ſo ſweet,

Saint Mary's Lake

And this old churchyard on the hill,
    That keeps the green graves of the dead,
So calm and sweet, so lone and still,
    And but the blue sky overhead.

Ah! here they lie, the simple race,
    Who lived their little flight of years,
Then laid them in this quiet place,
    At rest for ever from their fears.

The winds sing as they sang to them,
    The bracken changes as of old,
The hills still wear their diadem
    Of heather and the sunset's gold.

No change in these; the waves still break
    In ripple or in foam upon
The green shores of Saint Mary's Lake,
    As in the ages dead and gone.

Beneath the hills whose shadows seem
 Fit haunt for lonely sounds that be,
Flows, half in sunshine, Yarrow stream,
 The spirit of all I hear and see.

Thou Yarrow of my early dreams,
 When fancy heard thee murmur on,
A light has passed from other streams,
 And deepens all thy haunting tone.

It crowns thee with a magic dower;
 It makes thy windings ever sweet;
The Mary Scott of Dryhope Tower
 Still follows thee with unseen feet.

Her name is wed to thine; the vale
 Is witness as thou rollest on,
And with thee all the tender wail
 Of song, with sorrow in its tone.

Saint Mary's Lake

Men pafs from thee; the years prolong
  No name of theirs for ear or eye;
But fhe—a little whirl of fong
  Hath caught her, and fhe cannot die.

And, lying on the bracken'd hill,
  The funfhine on my brow, to-day,
The old Love-ballad echoes ftill
  In throbs that will not pafs away.

And as I liften, like a dream
  That changes into fofter things,
Saint Mary's Lake and Yarrow ftream
  Take all the forrow which it fings.

Alexander Anderfon.

L'ENVOI.

What time the merle and mavis sing,
We twine this Garland of the Spring:
The rose of Love, of roses chief,
Dark-blent with Sorrow's cypress-leaf,
And odorous violets, pensive-eyed,
And primrose of the green hillside:
Gathered from fields afar and near,
From western Brantwood's lovely mere.
From where the streets of London roar,
From distant Devon's classic shore,
From grey heights by the swelling Forth
Where sits the City of the North,
From Border vales that yield their fame
To his the Mighty Minstrel's name.
—If, in these buds and blossoms, aught
Should move thy mind to sweeter thought,
Or wake in thee thy better part,
Then, Reader, wear them on thy heart.

J. R.

www.ingramcontent.com/pod-product-compliance
Lightning Source LLC
Chambersburg PA
CBHW032245080426
42735CB00008B/1005